The World's **COOLEST** Jobs

TEST PILOT

Alix Wood

PowerKiDS
press

New York

Published in 2014 by The Rosen Publishing Group, Inc.
29 East 21st Street, New York, NY 10010

Editor for Alix Wood Books: Eloise Macgregor
Designer: Alix Wood
US Editor: Joshua Shadowens
Researcher: Kevin Wood
Military Consultant: Group Captain MF Baker MA RAF (Retd)
Educational Consultant: Amanda Baker BEd (Hons) PGCDL

Photo Credits: cover, 1, 7 bottom, 8, 9 top, 11 top, 17 top, 18, 19 top, 20 bottom, 28
© Defenseimagery.mil; 4, 14, 15, 17 bottom, 21 bottom, 22, 23, 25 top right, 29 ©
Shutterstock; 5, 9 bottom, 12, 13, 16 © MoD; 6, 7 top, 11 bottom, 21 top © public
domain; 10 © Dreamstime; 19, bottom © Carabás; 20 top © Finlay McWalter; 24, 25
top left © David Pryde; 25 bottom, 26, 27 bottom © NASA; 27 top © Jeff Foust

Library of Congress Cataloging-in-Publication Data

Wood, Alix.
 Test pilot / by Alix Wood.
    pages cm. — (The world's coolest jobs)
 Includes index.
 ISBN 978-1-4777-6019-2 (library) — ISBN 978-1-4777-6020-8 (pbk.) —
 ISBN 978-1-4777-6022-2 (6-pack)
 1. Test pilots—Vocational guidance—Juvenile literature. 2. Air pilots—Vocational
guidance—Juvenile literature. 3. Test pilots—Juvenile literature. 4. Airplanes—Flight
testing—Juvenile literature. 5. Hazardous occupations—Juvenile literature. I. Title.
 TL671.7W66 2014
 623.74'6048—dc23
                                2013026330

Manufactured in the United States of America

CPSIA Compliance Information: Batch #W14PK2: For Further Information contact Rosen Publishing, New York, New York at 1-800-237-9932

Contents

Test pilots fly new and **modified** aircraft. Their job is to see if the planes they test are safe and can do what they were designed to do. Test pilots may work for military organizations or private companies.

Test pilots need to be professional and precise. They need to understand the science behind why an aircraft flies and handles like it does. As well as flying the planes, they need to plan the test flight and decide how and what to test. They have to understand what they learned from the test and write reports.

A World War II Junkers aircraft crashed in Norway.

Testing military aircraft is the most risky flying done during peacetime. The job is demanding and dangerous. They need to decide if the planes are safe before anyone else uses them. To take a new aircraft up into the air for the very first time must be both exciting and terrifying.

👍 THAT'S COOL

Some test pilots are referred to as "golden arms." Some sports people are called golden arms if they have a good throw. A good test pilot needs to have a steady hand at the controls and be consistent, too.

FACT FILE

A test pilot must be able to:
- stick to a test plan, and fly the plane in a highly specific way
- have an excellent feel for the aircraft, and sense if it is behaving oddly
- fly to an above average standard
- have excellent **analytical** skills
- solve problems quickly if anything goes wrong
- cope with many things going wrong at once
- explain test observations to **engineers** and other pilots
- carefully document the results of each test
- understand **aeronautical** engineering

Early Pioneers

People began testing aircraft shortly before World War I. In the 1920s, test pilots worked for organizations such as the Royal Aircraft Establishment in the UK or the National Advisory Committee for Aeronautics in the United States, which later became NASA.

Léon Lemartin was the first ever test pilot. In 1910, he joined French **aviator** Louis Blériot's flying school to train as a pilot and work as an engineer. Blériot was famous for making the first flight across the English Channel in 1909. In February 1911, Lemartin broke a world record by carrying seven passengers in a Blériot XIII, breaking the previous record of six. He went on to increase the record to thirteen passengers. Lemartin died in an air race crash in June 1911.

An old postcard showing Lemartin carrying seven passengers in the Blériot XIII.

FACT FILE

Marina Popovich was a Russian test pilot who set many world records in aviation in the 1960s. She is one of the most famous pilots in Russian history, and one of the most important female pilots of all time.

Marina Popovich

Chuck Yeager was a fighter pilot during World War II, and then he became a test pilot. He tested many types of aircraft including experimental rocket-powered aircraft. In 1947, Yeager became the first pilot to travel faster than the speed of sound, known as **Mach** 1. He flew the experimental Bell X-1 at 670 miles per hour (1,078 km/h). He later broke Scott Crossfield's 1953 record of Mach 2, setting a new record of Mach 2.44!

A signed print showing Chuck Yeager in the Bell X-1, named Glamorous Glennis, after his wife.

Test Pilot Schools

There are a small number of specialist test pilot schools that train elite pilots to test **aerospace** weapons and aircraft. The test pilot schools don't just train the pilots. They train the flight test engineers and flight test **navigators**, too.

The United States Naval Test Pilot School (USNTPS) students include navy, marine, air force and army **officers**, civil service engineers, and students from other nations. The school is the only helicopter test pilot and engineer training school in the US. The USNTPS has an exchange program with the Air Force Test Pilot School in California, the Empire Test Pilot School in England, and the EPNER Test Pilot School in France. The exchanges enable the students to fly many more aircraft than they would be able to based at just one school.

United States Naval
Test Pilot School,
Maryland

8

A USNTPS Cayuse helicopter taking off on a training flight.

The schools teach about aircraft performance, stability and control, and systems testing. The **theory** is taught in the classroom, and then the students test out the theories in an airplane or helicopter. Teams learn how to draw up detailed test plans, test the aircraft in flight, analyze the results, and produce a report. Test pilot schools use a wide variety of aircraft. The students have to test the aircraft with its specific role in mind. A fighter is very different from a transport helicopter. The test pilot must understand the aircraft's role and design appropriate tests.

👍 THAT'S COOL

The oldest school is the Empire Test Pilots' School at MoD Boscombe Down in the UK. They train test pilots from around the world. It is a very tough but popular course. Usually three times as many people apply for the course than it has places for.

FACT FILE

After a test flight, the students have to write a long report on the aircraft and their findings and then present it to a room of senior officers. They must answer questions about their presentation and be confident about their answers.

Flight Simulators

Flight simulators artificially recreate the experience of being in an aircraft. The cockpits are identical, and they move and feel exactly like flying the real aircraft.

Test pilots get to know a new aircraft by spending hours in a flight simulator. A simulator can be programmed to mimic a particular aircraft. The controls are linked to computers that can generate different situations that a real aircraft would experience. They are very expensive to build, but at least they never crash!

 THAT'S COOL

Flight simulators make testing experimental new aircraft much less risky. Modifications can be tested out before a test flight.

A simulator is mounted on hydraulic legs that can move it about in any direction.

screen joint

The view from a simulator is very realistic. This Thunderbolt II flight simulator has three screens with visible joints. Some simulators now have one seamless visual system which wraps around the cockpit.

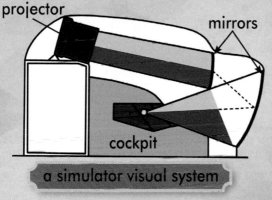

projector

mirrors

cockpit

a simulator visual system

In a modern specialist simulator, the wide-field visual system creates a very realistic flying experience. This "out-the-window" image is projected onto curved mirrored surfaces which wrap around the cockpit.

FACT FILE

The first known flight simulator (right) helped pilots fly the Antoinette monoplane. It was developed in 1909 to help pilots learn how to use the control wheels before flying the aircraft. Assistants would move the device using rods, depending on how the pilots used the control wheels.

This simulator was made from a barrel!

The Hawk T1

The Hawk T1 is an advanced training aircraft. Test pilot schools use a modified Hawk as a training tool. It is a very **versatile** aircraft.

The front cockpit is converted to make it behave a little like a flight simulator. The pupil sits in the front seat, and the instructor sits in the seat behind. From this rear seat, special controls enable the instructor to modify the aircraft to act like almost any other fast jet. The **center of gravity**, performance, and handling can all be changed so the Hawk T1 can react and feel just like flying an F-16 fighter jet!

A Royal Air Force (RAF) Hawk T1 jet aircraft on a training flight with a pilot and instructor.

FACT FILE

The UK's RAF aerobatic team, the Red Arrows, fly modified Hawks. The Hawks have a specialized engine and a modification that makes smoke trails. Diesel is mixed with a colored dye and ejected into the jet exhaust to produce either red, white, or blue smoke. Red Arrows pilots are all volunteers and have exceptional flying skills.

A Hawk T1 on the runway

230

👍 THAT'S COOL

The Hawk was designed specifically as a training aircraft. It can also be used as a single seater ground attack fighter or an air defense fighter armed with air-to-air missiles.

Life As a Test Pilot

There is no such thing as a typical day in the life of a test pilot. Some days are spent dealing with paperwork and some are spent flying new equipment up in the clouds.

The Federal Aviation Authority (FAA) employs test pilots to conduct flight tests on any new software. Once the equipment has been tested on the simulators, it arrives on the test pilot's desk. Flight testing is the final phase of testing. The pilot studies the test plan and talks it through with the team. They discuss the speed and height they should fly at. They decide on the specific way they need to fly, such as what angle the aircraft should bank at, and decide where the test flight should be done. On a flight day, the test pilot will talk to the maintenance and engineering crew and make sure the aircraft is ready.

Before the test flight, the team work out how much fuel is needed, and check what the weather will be like.

👍 THAT'S COOL

Test pilots often fly
through the toughest
weather. They will test fly
in Alaska in mid-winter when
the temperature is below
-4° F (-20° C), or fly to
the South Pacific during a
heatwave. They like to test
in crosswinds during the
gale season, too. Severe
weather conditions really
test the aircraft.

FACT FILE

Test pilots need to keep fit. Some test pilots
will fly two **sorties** a day, and each flight
can be a few hours long. Test pilots often
experience **g-forces**. G-forces put strain on
a pilot's body when flying at top speed. "G"
stands for gravity, which pulls objects toward
Earth. Normal gravity is 1 G. A test pilot
can experience over 6 G. At 6 G, the pilot
will seem six times heavier, find it hard to
breathe, and may black out. Training, oxygen,
and special "pressure pants," which stop the
blood from pooling in the legs, all help to
fight this danger. During testing the aircraft
can also roll 360 degrees per second, and
physical fitness is necessary just to stay
conscious in the cockpit.

Military Test Pilots

Military test pilots get to fly a great many different and exciting aircraft. It is a dangerous job. It is important that new military equipment is tested thoroughly. It must be able to do what it was designed for and be as safe as possible.

Military test pilots are in a more vulnerable environment than virtually any other type of pilot. They must remain constantly aware of all emergency procedures and be ready to act quickly in a crisis. The job is both physically demanding and produces a great deal of mental stress and fatigue.

A Chinook helicopter on a test flight, with a flight test navigator and test pilot on board.

A tailspin is the rapid, uncontrolled descent of an aircraft in a steep spiral. Military test pilots put aircraft into a spin to check the plane's ability to recover from one. This is a very dangerous procedure. Anti-spin parachutes can be shot from the tail of the aircraft which stabilize the spin by causing drag. Small rockets under the wings can also stop the aircraft from rotating. **Transmitters** can be placed on an aircraft before spin testing enabling a pilot on the ground to analyze the situation and advise the pilot in the aircraft on the best ways to recover the plane.

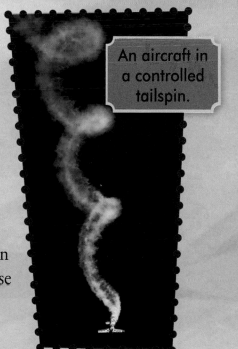

An aircraft in a controlled tailspin.

Testing the F-35 Lightning II

The F-35 is a new fighter being developed for the US and UK military. As it is a joint project between different countries, the test pilots have to do a lot of traveling.

Test flying a F-35 is very different from flying any other aircraft. It is controlled by voice command or by using a touchscreen panel. The advanced software can diagnose mechanical problems and radio information to ground crews. All the new equipment had to be rigorously tested.

👍 THAT'S COOL

The F-35B can take off on a very short runway, and can land vertically. The plane hovers by using a powerful fan. The pilot can gradually lower it to the runway.

an F-35 Lightning II (center) and two F-16 Fighting Falcons

The F-35 has a very different cockpit design from any previous aricraft. Instead of hundreds of switches and dials, it has a 20 inch (60 cm) touchscreen display. Pilots customize the screen to show what they need to see at any one time. With a specially designed helmet that links to the control panel, the pilot can turn his head and still see the information displayed in green in the photo (right). With so many linked pieces of equipment to test, this was a complicated project.

What the pilot sees through the visor

F-35 cockpit

FACT FILE

The helmet displays information on the visor of the helmet that the pilot wears. This means important information is always in the pilot's line of sight. The pilot can launch weapons simply by looking at the target. Everyone's eyes are different. The helmet has to be adjusted to fit the space between each pilot's eyes, for instance. The depth of the display can be adjusted to suit the pilot, too. The pilot can assess the information on the screen and the information in the line of sight at the same time, effectively able to look in two directions at once!

A test pilot wearing a helmet with the helmet mounted display.

Black Projects

A black project is a highly **classified** secret military project. Test pilots may help to develop top secret aircraft and security will be tight.

A warning sign at Area 51, in the Nevada desert.

guarding a B-2 bomber

The B-2 Spirit stealth bomber (below) was developed in secrecy. The project was highly classified and the military denied its existence until the aircraft was fully ready. The secrecy led to several reported **UFO** sightings in the testing area as no one had seen such an unusual aircraft in the sky before! It can be necessary to develop defense systems in secrecy to stop other countries from copying or learning how to combat the new design.

The A-12 was a **reconnaissance** aircraft built in secret for the Central Intelligence Agency (CIA). When one crashed in 1963 a cover story was invented that a different type of aircraft had crashed, and witnesses were paid not to discuss what they had seen.

The unusual-shaped A-12

👍 **THAT'S COOL**

The first US military jet aircraft was disguised with a fake propeller when parked on the airfield. One pilot is said to have even flown wearing a gorilla suit, to convince other pilots who saw the aircraft flying that they were seeing things!

The secrecy surrounding the Nevada Test and Training Range, known as Area 51, has made it the frequent subject of **conspiracy theories** and UFO sightings. Reports of UFOs and even a disappearing airstrip have been rumored to have been sighted at Area 51. Some people believe Area 51 stores and examines crashed alien spacecraft and studies their occupants, for example. The secrecy necessary to protect the development of military equipment can lead to some fairly strange stories as people try to make sense of what they see.

Commercial Airline Testing

Production test pilots fly every aircraft as it comes off the assembly line at the factory. Airline test pilots test airliners after major overhauls as well.

Imagine flying thousands of feet (m) up in the air and then having to shut off and restart the engines on a gigantic airliner. That is what commercial airline test pilots do routinely as they test their aircraft.

Two commercial airline test pilots check through the test plan before take off.

When testing a commercial aircraft, it is usually stripped back and most of the seats are taken out. The cabin is filled with scientific equipment to measure and record what happens on the flight. The results can then be analyzed later. The aircraft is tested in a number of conditions, such as high altitudes and extreme weather.

👍 THAT'S COOL

Test pilots may be testing something as tiny as a new indicator light, or as large as the emergency back-up systems. Test pilots have to undertake dangerous procedures, such as shutting down and relighting each engine mid-flight.

FACT FILE

Math can be very important to test pilots, because it helps them understand why airplanes behave the way they do. Test pilots do carefully planned tests in a new airplane to work out how to balance a load. Their results help airlines to know the best way to load passengers, for example. The tests involve complicated math to predict how a plane will fly under certain conditions. Test pilots then go out and test the aircraft and find out if their math was right!

Airlines don't seat passengers together at the front or the back of the aircraft. Passengers are spread out so the plane is balanced. Otherwise the plane becomes a lot harder for the pilots to fly.

The Beluga Airbus

Being a test pilot on a project such as the Beluga Airbus is challenging. The wings, engines, landing gear, and lower part of the **fuselage** are the same as the Airbus 300. However, the upper fuselage has an enormous cargo area which alters the handling of the aircraft dramatically.

To provide access to the cargo area from the front, the Airbus 300 cockpit had to be moved downward. The tail structure was enlarged and strengthened to make the aircraft more stable. Test pilots had to help work out what changes were needed to balance the aircraft so it could fly safely.

👍 THAT'S COOL

The picture below shows a Beluga Airbus loading NH-90 helicopters on the runway in Canberra, Australia. The Beluga's freight compartment is an amazing 123.7 feet (37.7 m) long!

The aircraft is named after the beluga whale (right) because of its similarity in looks!

The Beluga was built to transport Airbus parts. Because building the Airbus is a joint project between various countries, large aircraft parts needed to be flown around the world. Test pilots had to test the aircraft to establish what its **payload** could be, and how to store loads in the cargo bay. After 335 hours of test flying, the Beluga entered service.

FACT FILE

Belugas have been used to carry other special loads, including space station components and large paintings. The Beluga was intended for large but relatively light cargo. The maximum payload is 51.8 tons (47 t), compared to the smaller military transport aircraft, the C-5 Galaxy, which can carry 135 tons (122.5 t).

The *Columbus* science laboratory being unloaded at Kennedy Space Center.

Test Pilots and Space

Neil Armstrong, the first man to set foot on the moon, used to be a test pilot in the 1950s. Many astronauts are chosen from the ranks of military test pilots. Astronauts and test pilots have many similar qualities.

When British army test pilot Tim Peake was selected to join the International Space Station, he said that he thought his future career would probably be safer than his past career, having carried out some fairly risky flight tests! Test pilots are chosen as astronauts because they are used to dealing with emergencies under stressful conditions and are familiar with the physical and mental stress of high-speed flight in unproven aircraft. The pilots of the first human spaceflight program in the United States, called Project Mercury, were all military test pilots with strong engineering backgrounds.

Test pilot Neil Armstrong with his X-15 rocket powered aircraft after a research flight in 1960.

FACT FILE

A new type of space program is being planned by an airline. They plan to provide space flights for space tourists. After an intense selection process from some of the best pilots in the world, they chose former US Air Force test pilot Keith Colmer as the first astronaut pilot. Many famous names have already bought tickets to be passengers on the flights!

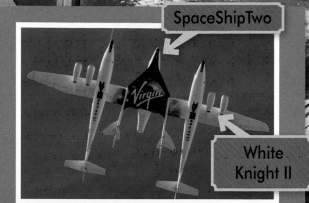

SpaceShipTwo

White Knight II

Virgin Galactic's SpaceShipTwo will be launched from the twin hull aeroplane White Knight II.

Astronauts help maintain the International Space Station.

👍 THAT'S COOL

The pilot of a space shuttle must have flown 1,000 hours as a jet pilot before they can be selected as an astronaut.

Still Want To Be a Test Pilot?

Being a test pilot is a challenging job. It takes determination to be good enough to be selected. Test pilots need to be analytical and to be able to think under pressure. It can be stressful.

To be considered as a test pilot you need to be physically fit. You need to first become a professional pilot, either as a civilian or by joining the military. You also need to have an advanced qualification in aeronautical engineering, and be excellent at physics and maths. It is expensive to go to a test pilot school, and civilian pilots will often be sponsored by an airline who pay the bill. The military pay the bill for military students.

A test pilot climbs out of an A-10 Thunderbolt II aircraft

There are plenty of good points about being a test pilot. Test pilots earn a very good salary. They usually work a regular 40 hour week and generally get to fly one day a week, depending on what kind of aircraft they are testing. Bad points are that sometimes the job can involve last minute travel. If the weather conditions somewhere become perfect for testing, test pilots may have to fly off at a moment's notice. After months of planning a test it is very exciting to step up to the aircraft for a test flight. Test pilots feel privileged that they can fly the plane they helped to create.

FACT FILE

Planning and paperwork are very important. One of the skills of a test pilot is that they work really hard to make test flights as boring as possible! A thorough planning stage stops emergencies from happening.

Glossary

aeronautical
(er-oh-NAW-tih-kul)
Relating to the science dealing with the operation of aircraft.

aerospace (ER-oh-spays)
The earth's atmosphere and the space beyond.

analytical (a-nuh-LIH-tih-kul)
Skilled in using analysis.

aviator (AY-vee-ay-tur)
A pilot.

center of gravity
(SEN-tur UV GRA-vuh-tee)
The point at which an object is in balance.

classified (KLAS-uh-fyd)
Withheld from the knowledge of the general public for reasons of national security.

conspiracy theories
(kun-SPEER-uh-see THEER-eez)
Theories that explain an event as being the result of a secret plot.

engineers (en-juh-NEERZ)
Designers or builders of engines.

fuselage (FYOO-seh-lahzh)
The central body portion of an airplane.

g-forces (GEE-fors-ez)
The force of gravity or acceleration on a body.

Mach (MAHK)
The ratio of the speed of a body to that of sound in the surrounding medium.

modified (MAH-dih-fyd)
Altered from its original state.

navigators (NA-vuh-gay-turz)
People responsible for directing the course in a ship or aircraft.

payload (PAY-lohd)
Cargo carried by a vehicle.

reconnaissance
(ree-CON-ih-sens)
A survey (as of enemy territory) to gain information.

sorties (SOR-teez)
Moves against an enemy.

theory (THEER-ee)
The general ideas or principles of a subject.

transmitters (tranz-MIT-urz)
Devices that send out radio or television signals.

UFO (YOO-ef-oh)
An unidentified flying object, such as an alien spaceship.

versatile (VUR-suh-tyl)
Able to do many different kinds of things.

WEBSITES

Due to the changing nature of Internet links, PowerKids Press has developed an online list of websites related to the subject of this book. This site is updated regularly. Please use this link to access the list:

www.powerkidslinks.com/wcj/pilot

Read More

Clark, Willow. *Planes On the Move*. Transportation Station. New York: PowerKids Press, 2010.

Martin, Ted. *Area 51*. The Unexplained. Minneapolis, MN: Bellwether Media, Inc., 2011.

Shea, Therese. *Spy Planes*. Military Machines. New York: Gareth Stevens Learning Library, 2013.

Index